# Pearl sighting, a rare sighting

Pramod Kesav N

Notion Press

# NOTION PRESS

India. Singapore. Malaysia.

This book has been published with all reasonable efforts taken to make the material error-free after the consent of the author. No part of this book shall be used, reproduced in any manner whatsoever without written permission from the author, except in the case of brief quotations embodied in critical articles and reviews.

The Author of this book is solely responsible and liable for its content including but not limited to the views, representations, descriptions, statements, information, opinions and references ["Content"]. The Content of this book shall not constitute or be construed or deemed to reflect the opinion or expression of the Publisher or Editor. Neither the Publisher nor Editor endorse or approve the Content of this book or guarantee the reliability, accuracy or completeness of the Content published herein and do not make any representations or warranties of any kind, express or implied, including but not limited to the implied warranties of merchantability, fitness for a particular purpose. The Publisher and Editor shall not be liable whatsoever for any errors, omissions, whether such errors or omissions result from negligence, accident, or any other cause or claims for loss or damages of any kind, including without limitation, indirect or consequential loss or damage arising out of use, inability to use, or about the reliability, accuracy or sufficiency of the information contained in this book.

# Foreword

This book, Pearl sighting, a rare sighting draws parallels on the widening gap between English speaking writers who are domiciled in the different parts of the world.

In reality, it conveys the rigid path a Foreign service officer from India with a literature background may encounter when in service in the localities and small towns in places like North America, England, and India.

Also, in this work, a basic but formal literary analysis is attempted in figuring out the profound influences wielded by eminent world statesmen, and politicians, who were active in the last decade of the twentieth century and towards the beginning of the millennium. Events which are related and relate to famous English literary figures, and characters are depicted where-ever explanations are sought in such an analysis.

It is a hope that the reader is well informed about generation labels, and the events that unfold in the contemporary period, with significant focus on what lied ahead for each of them literally, in the Victorian periods to the digital ages of today.

Hope this work is an easy read for the literature enthusiasts and others.

Pramod Kesav N

(Payikkattu, Kalavamkodam, Cherthala, Alappuzha, Kerala, India)

# Preface

Pearl sighting, a rare sighting is a book that holds a few answers to the key concerns in the current generation and it tries to reveal some of the important events that happened in the past right in the Victorian period to the digital ages of today, in particular lies the attack on the World Trade centre (9/11) in the year 2001.

When we go still back in history to the last century, we have had two world wars, followed by a cold war and the developments henceforth as many know is that the Allies led by US and UK fought against the Axis powers led by Germany and Japan, ultimately defeating the Axis powers, when it finally concluded.

An event of significant importance was the Japanese attack on Pearl Harbour which is US territory, which brought in the United States of America to wage the World War (II) against the Axis powers.

Several such events had happened even after the world wars culminated and wars continued in different parts of the world, mainly in the form of Cold war between the United States and the Soviet Union.

Several things have in fact happened during this long period in history, which is a century long period.

There was rise of the Communist bloc (led by the Soviet Union) of countries in Eastern Europe that were in war footage with the Western bloc led by the US.

Several decades later we also saw the crumbling of the Berlin wall which ultimately united East Germany and West Germany.

In this work, an attempt is made to see the developments in the world of English literature, which is more a basic treatment given to the events that unfold in remotest places in England or its vassals and its principalities by taking inspiration from contributions from the English literary figures, providing convincing but meaningful explanations of related events, and happening.

Hope you have an easy read on this topic.

Thanks for all your continued support.

Pramod Kesav N (Author)

# Contents

Off one goes

to break veil and

to acquaint oneself

with the literary plot

# 1

## Mean, Greedy, and the explorative sense

Going mean is nasty and it evokes a humiliating experience to one another, however hard one tries, being greedy at the same time is again adventurous in overtures and actions which may pump up residual energy possibly resulting in a wandering thought.

The thought of an explorative sense.

That is when it started going for the confused state of mind which met with an unfamiliar terrain and only a question remained.

What if all the characters of a cartoon series have a mind of their own making?

It then becomes mean, greedy, and perfect nonsense that would restate a few intelligent buffs but the sane mind keeps on wandering...

**Animated sitcom and the favourite characters**

The favourite thus far is The Simpsons.

For the benefit of those who are not television geeks, some explanations are provided.

Matt Groening created a very famous American animated sitcom called as The Simpsons, which is a sitcom with its satirical rendering of the American life, symbolized by the

Simpson family consisting of Homer, Marge, Bart, Lisa, and Maggie with more characters of whom, one of the sidekicks, a form of a toon character is Francesca Terwilliger.

She is the Italian wife of Robert Terwilliger (Sideshow Bob) and the mother of Gino Terwilliger, appears in the episode titled: The Italian Bob, where the Simpson family encounters Sideshow Bob living in Italy with his new family.

Some form of brief explanations can be given about some of the main characters so that one can become familiar with the toon characters of the sitcom: The Simpsons.

Homer is the patriarch of the family and is married to Marge and has three children.  As the family's income earner, he works as a safety inspector at the Springfield Nuclear power plant. He is overweight, lazy, outspoken, and ignorant.

Marge Simpson is a central character from The Simpsons and her role is that of a mother of the Simpson family and wife of Homer Simpson.  She is the mother to Bart, Lisa, and Maggie. She is most recognizable by her tall blue beehive hairstyle and her dress which is usually green, and wears a sensible shoe and red necklace. Though she embodies in the role of a traditional homemaker, she is pictured as a one who held various jobs, that of a police officer, realtor, and a pretzel vendor. She comes from the Bouvier family with sisters Selma, and Patty who are often critical of Homer where Marge's unwavering loyalty to Homer is always a recurring theme in the sitcom.

## Some explanations on Cultured Pearl

Are natural pearls in the decline to the point of getting exhausted from the face of the earth?

Yes, the answer is correct, natural pearls are in a significant decline and very rare to the point they are quite exhausted from their natural habitats in the Persian Gulf, Red Sea, Indian Ocean near Sri Lanka and India, and in the Gulf of Mannar.

Due to intense harvesting, habitat destruction, and pollution, destruction of natural pearls drastically reduced wild oyster population.

Pearl diving was unsustainable and intense in the Persian Gulf, and India in the early 1990, where in one attempt, divers collected every oyster, regardless of its size, or maturity which brought down the natural pearl population in the sea bed.

Sedimentation and Pollution further reduced and destroyed natural habitat for pearls, especially mangroves, and coral reefs where many natural pearl producing oysters lived.

In Japan, in the early 1990s, cultured pearls were invented by Mikimoto, which involved human induced seeding, producing pearls faster and with more reliability.  Now, the Japanese dominate this industry, with nearly all the pearls in the market being cultured pearl, in place of natural pearls which used to be there adoring jewellery, made out of platinum, and gold.

## Somewhere a Cultured Pearl jeopardized a Cultural Pearl

Recently a cultural Pearl could not stand the humiliation when it was told that it stands with a cultured Pearl.  The beast, a domestic cat was mewing all over, the way it was mewing was more like a grumble from its master or is it its mistress when it was told that the ornament it was wearing was man made, induced artificially by the Japanese, since the original ones are not any more available from the deepest oceans and the roughest barriers.

The mistress a cultural plight seemingly in her forties resembled a real dignitary and was absolutely fair in complexion and wore mostly platinum jewellery immediately wanted to hush her pet. Her flamboyance was utterly a waste of efforts and took the name of a Francesca Terwilliger.

It is still a lot of answers in anvil if somebody puts her name to be the female counterpart of a Francis, whose origin is from Italy, an Italian name, a Francesca, in short, Francesca Terwilliger.

Somebody nearby them exclaimed that usually the cat mews whenever it sees a tomcat and the tomcat mews in a so called, yowl or caterwaul when it spots a real beast.

So, you see it is quite contagious, what are the emotions, a feeling of let-down, let alone fear in the middle of flamboyance, the fear of being rejected all over, whether it is from a beast or from a genuine human bigwig.

Pearl sighting, a rare sighting

Before getting on with the worries of any cultural pearl, they always thought their cat always looked at the king, in simple words, a cat who may look at a king.

To understand it better, one should understand how it is to feel humiliated in front of a superior power, the cat surely felt it, it knew the cultured pearl was no match for the natural pearl which is no more available, that its ornaments took a deep dive in terms of its quality and the grandeur it is supposed to have held.

Even a person of humble status does not have to humiliate or grovel himself in the presence of a superior power, Francesca Terwilliger, the mistress doesn't get it, the cat thinks?

Yes, the cultural pearl does not get it?

So, who is this cultural pearl?  What is so special about her?

We do not know yet.

We know one thing for sure, a cultural pearl is more than a metaphor a term hopefully one can call a person who is someone of a greater cultural value.

So, is the cat mistaken?

Does its master, a genuine form of its mistress, so completely oblique?

Somebody told, Oblique, did they tell Obelix?

Well, Obelix is the sidekick of Asterix, the Gaul, a cartoon character created by Rene Goscinny, and Albert Uderzo. He is well known for his super human powers and he is the go getter for all menhir for all trade, whatever is now left there, and who loves eating boar and keeps hitting bewildered Roman soldiers.

But nowhere, we can draw any similes, neither can we utter a remote semblance to the very creativity that its creators pour into the making of those cartoon characters by those renowned American creators like, Matt Groening.

Has anybody thought, what it is to barge into their homes, with Homer, Marge, Bart, Lisa, Meggie, and Appu?  They are all very gay in Springfield, which is the town they hail from. But still it is not like any Terwilliger, so such horrible demeanour in the cat's mistress that can never be bestowed upon her, that the Simpson's team despite their creativity still had to take criticisms all around while passing through their Golden age to getting on with their periods of criticisms.

The first criticism was on the cameo like appearances often offered by those big Halliday characters, who was criticized is no small amount for reflecting real-life circumstances.

It might have diminished the whole point of The Simpsons show, says some because it mixed some elements of reality show being the subject of a greater tumult with the showcasing of American life which otherwise would have been normally expressed through a cartoon's perspective.

So, was Ms. Terwilliger had a genuine cultured pearl for her to be called a cultural pearl?  Was she still trying to own a natural pearl, we do not know.

Now to get on with the next criticism that The Simpson must take.

It is for a Mike Sully.

Mike Sully was criticized for completing seasons 9 till 12 and the subject of criticisms were vocal more like under Sully's tenor, the critics were at a Homer blowing a tranquilizer dart into Marge's neck.

The critics were at it, at the scene, and argued that scenes like this, would depict domestic violence as humour, thereby mimicking real life balance of events as a chance to display the abuse of some persons over others for wielding personal control.

In short, they did not like themes of violence, normalization of abuse and gender dynamics that were not balanced in the characters interplay and in its attempt of balancing personal relationship, introduction or usage of violence was largely seen as a deviant behaviour quite not expected of a show like The Simpsons.

So, here again we are left with a Ms. Terwilliger not actually understanding what is expected of her, when her cat disapproves being humiliated for not wearing the best ornament and not being aware of sighting a pearl, a natural one, of what used to be worn by the haves and not the have-nots.

Humiliating oneself is such a scenario before a superior power is a grovelling experience?

Let us see...

Let's take taxi drivers for instance, and that too from London...

Usually, the taxi drivers in London or the London cabbies are known to be very knowledgeable because some of the philosophical questions posed by them could not be answered by famous philosophers themselves.

In one instance, a debate was all inclusive, in particular when one considered a long-standing debate, a philosophical debate for instance, where in a lighter sense in a philosopher's theoretical knowledge was put to test against a taxi driver's practical knowledge.

In the past, such debates have occurred, like the one with Betrand Russel, where some questions that were asked by the taxi drivers could not be answered by Russel in deed emphasizing the difficulty of getting simple and readily applicable answers distilled into philosophical ideas.

Hence it was surmised that the taxi drivers could not what Russel himself could not answer in philosophical terms to questions asked by the same taxi drivers.

So, was it a humiliating experience for the philosopher?

That can only be answered after inspecting the varied visuals and based on the dialogs that the philosopher conveys when asked in person.

Several American writers, particularly the ones who lived or spent time in New York City have described surprisingly philosophical discussions that they had with taxi drivers and they describe the conversations with them as profound, it not anything else!

Serving literary or a symbolic purpose, many authors have spoken seriously about the cab driver's insights, especially in a city like the New York City, filled with immigrants and their complex lives.

One of the notable persons who has commented on this subject is Charles Simic, the Pulizer prize winning poet who exclaimed that the taxi drivers of New York especially the immigrants are a philosophical bunch of people and gave a whole new perspective to taxi riding in the city.

Another notable writer, Cole has described it interesting walking and taking cab rides through the New York City and Teju says cab drivers give a perspective reflective of the city's layered consciousness.

Now what if there was a dignitary who wanted to just visit NOAA or the National Oceanic and Atmospheric Administration in the Cooperative Science Center in New York?

Do they allow it if it is out of a touristic interest?

Not sure.

But did somebody say Seismology?

Let us see if or who lost the credit?

**Give Credit where the Credit is due?**

United Kingdom in collaboration with the United States operated a network of seismic monitoring stations which were capable of detecting seismic activities particularly those conducted by the erst Soviet Union in the Eastern Bloc of countries.  These efforts were spearheaded by the

United Kingdom in an effort to monitor compliances with nuclear test bans which were in force and to gather intelligence on nuclear activities during the Cold War.

Several Seismic monitoring stations were set during that time period from 1966 to 1970 in various part of the world including Eskdale Muir in Scotland, Warumungu in Australia, Yellowknife in Canada, and Gauribidanur Seismic Array (GBA) in Karnataka, India.

These stations were equipped with seismographs capable of detecting seismic waves from activities that may not only limit itself to underground nuclear explosions.  These very data that were collected using the seismology equipment were shared with international monitoring organizations and made sure countries complied with nuclear test ban treaties.

Though it did not control any nuclear explosions that happened during or afterwards in many countries, who went ahead with declaring themselves nuclear powers, it at the minimum reported who were those powers who were capable of holding nuclear arms which gave into fresh treatises, in that regard.

Any seismology related activities taken up by the United Kingdom is usually monitored by British Geological Survey which is a department operating under Operating the UK National Seismograph Network (UKNSN).

All these efforts by the UK seismology departments were taken note of by the general public in UK, USA, and the rest of the world during that time period that there were criticisms that emerged out of many renowned authors from during that time.

In 1968 a popular work Rock Baby was released whose author M Woodhouse felt that a personified character, personification on a continent country was not half as daft as what he thought and he only wanted due credit to be extended to the Isles.

Even-though it was also published as Bush Baby in the US, the connotations varied quite a bit in matters that was presented to the US readers, to the extent they started getting a totally different impression about the book. Many in the US commented that UK was carrying out the seismograph's installations illegally in many parts of the world, with reference to the character Woodhouse quoting excerpts from the book Wilt by T Sharpe who also called him a maniac in the year 1976.

So, this sort of literary renditions went on within the Western Bloc in its numerous literary classes both in the US and in the UK, let alone in other parts of the world and give rise to likely debates in support or contentious to the actual subject in question, which was that, due credit to the British isles were not given for its seismological installations in the different parts of the world.

However, in the year 2002, SAIF SAREEA 2 was carried out by the UK defence department with the Sultanate of Oman was one of the largest military exercises conducted by the United Kingdom in recent decades and the biggest deployment of British forces since the 1982 Falklands war was a coveted operation, which brought in much attention and appreciation to the UK defence department.

In the same year, an article that appeared in the Washington Post expressed gratitude to the readers and conveyed that it gave credit when its due, even when it is not, and considered it a fair deal even if it is localized to just the deserts.

# 2

## History repeats itself as a story of the victors

Through leading disciplined lives, humans tend to record developments in the various fields which are political, scientific, administrative, ... and in that venture, the record of events at some point in time gives a historical record of events.

Now to interpret that or reinterpret is a call made by the historians but the interest here is not to see how the events are recorded but to refute if not do anything else, the righteousness behind recording history as a story of the victorious side.

**Refuting History from the victorious viewpoint**

In some sense history when used by critical theorists has a complicated and contested meaning though the concept may seem straight forward.

For the most of us, the history that we now know today is really a recent development of the 19th century explained by Hayden White.

In his books Meta History (1973) and the Content of the Form (1987), White illustrates the extent to which history as a subject, a discipline borrows from narratives and general forms, to make those accounts into a historical record.

This is also specifically mentioned in the works, The Archetype of Romance, Comedy, Tragedy, and Satire (1973).

In the end (and throughout his works), he questions the concept of historical lessons to be no different than forms that previous annuls and chronicles suggest, as a sequence without beginnings or as a sequence that ends but never concludes, more or less suggesting that history is an ongoing affair.

One of the early influences on reconceptualization of history is the Frankfurt school which questioned traditional history because of its tendency to tell stories of the past from the perspective of the victors and to get the past in a narrative of cause and effect.

In essence, the Frankfurt school theorists go to the extent questioning Karl Max's own grand narratives of historical progression and economic determination on the premises that historicism moves around itself by establishing causal connections between various historical moments, thereby becoming historical, posthumously as if it were through events separated by hundred if not by thousands of years.

In short, it is urged that rather than tell the story of the victors, a historical materialist according to Walter Benjamin (Frankfurt School) one must brush history against the grain for the true depository of history, according to him is not man or men but the struggling oppressed classes.

And in essence, this would make a historian not tell the story of the victors but let the continuum of history explode and by conveying history as a state of emergency which is constant and often beaten up by the same ones who records it.

This in particular gains ground because everywhere opposing forces and discourses are constantly struggling for dominance where potential revolution constantly struggles against exploitation and oppression.

Otherwise called as an Approach, followed by British Cultural materialists, they also study the mission where analysis is done on how hegemonic forces in a culture seek to marginalize and disenfranchise the oppressed.

They rather than examine history from the above or the victorious history, but also identify competing forces in a given timeframe.

This is hence what is given in his works by Raymond William who influentially suggest history should not only consider dominant hegemonic forces in a given time period but also the residual and emergent forces that offer groups the possibility to counter hegemonic formats in dynamics forming dominant, residual, and emergent (forces).

## What lies ahead for a Marino Francesca?

Now in the footholds of a successful author, Marino in her work Baluchistan Bruised, Battered, and Bloodied, the intent of her writing is very clear as the work serves as a poignant expose of a systematic oppression faced by the Baluch people under Pakistan's rule.

Through meticulous research and first-hand accounts, Marino illuminates strategic interests with the regions complex history and brings out the traits of some leaders that severe human rights leading to its violation often endured by the Baluch people.

Throughout her book, she urges her readers to acknowledge the plight of Baloch people and advocates for international intervention to address injustices faced by several of them and the work stands as a testament to the resilience of Baloch people and reminder to the global community of where they should uphold the fundamental human rights.

Her book has been recognised for its emotional resilience and of its in-depth analysis where it is mentioned by its readers and the reading community that Marino excelled in her comprehensive approaches of drawing contemporary issues when they get blended with a lot of historical contexts.

## Francesca Terwilliger in the imaginary state of Phil-Einstein

Reasonably placed placards moved across the streets of Amsterdam. There is a hullabaloo in the surrounding places, streets with pavements leading to easy exits.  A lot of policemen play guard to the entrance and exit ways of the city's metro networks.

Prejudiced some said but a lot of shouting were heard in the form of slogans and it was going stronger and the junta increasing its count by numbers, now seemingly a common sight in the busy streets.

And in the middle of them all, in a quite unassuming attire emerges (as in a hybrid film where toons and real characters coexist) the toon character Francesca Terwilliger in quite a new reincarnation.  This time she is all dressed up well and on a trip to the ancient state in the Middle East, as adept personality qualified with a lot of educational degree from Universities like the SOAS London, where she in the first screen, quite wholeheartedly admits that she loves adoring pizza.

Recently appointed as a Rapporteur in what remains as a country, in the ancient state which lies in the southern coast of the imaginary Phil-Einstein, she was tasked to do many things to make life easier for the Phil-Einsteins.

In her immediate days of appointment, very many things, she wanted to do, though her role in the previous incarnation as Francesa, which did give her all the strength and did not undermine her strengths in giving out proclamations and warnings.

She was seen to make warnings, in a few instances, she warned that the region which the ancient Phil-Einsteins occupied would be the subject of ethnic cleansing someday, also she wanted an end to Apartheid and wanted a global summit in support of that and thought that the ancient people would give up on bows and arrows, a sense of a ceasefire which she would mediate, pushing the warring factions to give up on the war entirely.

It is not yet known whether she was successful in any of these but she set forth with this and while doing so at the minimum she should keep somethings in mind.

As we all know, she takes reincarnations, many in numbers.

So, whenever Francesca takes new incarnations, she should get out of a supporting role, in other words she should outlive the hangover of her supporting role in the cartoon, The Simpsons mindset and should drive the political conditions in such a way that the others may offer her lead roles in many other cartoons.

Mission accomplished in the land of Phil-Einstein, now she as in the toon character, Francesca Terwilliger wants to head towards a place called London, where from she can time-travel with the help of a transponder to a haunted place called The Pall Mall Magazine, in the time frame from 1874 to 1916.

**Historical context from the conquered people**

Elaborating on Baruch Halpern's book David's Secret Demons, it offers a provocative reassessment of King David, by challenging portrayals that are biblical in nature. Halpern being a prominent Jewish scholar, employed a multi-disciplinary approach combining textual criticisms, archaeology, and historical analysis reconstructed a complex but controversial image of King David.

Halpern opposes the general belief that the biblical narratives render in Samuel as a form of royal propaganda, crafted to legitimize the reign of David and that of his son Solomon.  He suggests that the text in the biblical verses were rendered by Solomon's scribes, aiming to portray David in a favourable light by suppressing any negative aspects of his rule.  By examining the biblical text through the lens of David's potential adversaries, Halpern reconstructs and portrays David as an opportunist, mercenary, and a political manipulator.

## Portrayal of David

Halpern thinks that the David portrayed in Bible may have been a Canaanite mercenary rather than an Israelite, possibly serving under King Achish of Gath (Philistine King). This argument of Halpern puts him in direct conflict and in a challenging position to the traditional view that David was the divinely chosen leader of Israel.

## Manoeuvring of David in the Political landscape

Halpern thinks the biblical king David as a figure who used assassinations and alliances to ascend the throne and power.  Halpern argues that David may have been responsible for the deaths of figures like Ishbosheth, Amasa, and Abner all of whom were from Saul's lineage.

## The Bathsheba Incident

Halpern thinks the story of David's affair with Bathsheba merely solidifies the argumentative note that it was not merely a moral failing on the part of King David but part of a broader pattern of manipulation, and exploitation.

Critics of Halpern's work conveyed mixed reaction where some of them praise his thorough research, and innovative approaches while other criticises his conclusions, as well as his methods, though many claim them questionable.

Herbert H Klement a scholar has reviewed Baruch Halpern's book, David's Secret Demons and in his review, he criticises Halpern for the approach that Halpern has taken to biblical scholarship and his portrayal of King David.

Klement argues that the interpretation that Halpern gives to King David, as a "serial killer" and figure who often is manipulative, even-though comes from Halpern's methodical approach is overly critical and dismissive of narratives that are biblical in nature.

Though Klement dismisses Halpern's work as more speculative than factual, he also suggests that Halpern's work reflects a broader trend in biblical scholarship that undermines traditional interpretation of biblical phrases and figures.

Klement's concern is about the approaches that Halpern takes in his work may erode foundational understanding of biblical text that deviates historical interpretation of facts that may have followed from the biblical era.

In summary, Herbert H Klement's criticisms of Baruch Halpern's book: David's Secret Demons centres around speculation on King David's portrayal as well as over-interpretations that might have broader implication on biblical scholarships.

# 3

## Homer sometimes nods like a homeless

Francesca Terwilliger from the cartoon show, The Simpsons is on an onward journey, this time to the countless Boroughs of New Jersey where she intends to settle down a little bit and visit some homes.

A home gets some of the homies occasionally and the bonding keeps some of them prosper, some of them falter and some merely ends up being hello-hello friends right from within the million-dollar neighbourhoods to the middle-income dwells to the external extents of those dweller or the slum, is definitely one thing to be taken note of.

Now, imagine what if an entire neighbourhood imaginary of course, near Utopia living communities in Cresskill, NJ, US, willingly and mostly owe to a common habit that they inculcated or subsumed or consumed, of that of smoking intoxicated substance, transformed their lives to homie neighbourhoods on streets, sidewalks and the harsh realities of an asylum.

It is a pity of what drives them to such obscure habits only to reincarnate into dozy living and hopeless might that many live to the point, nobody can have a meaningful dialog with some such.

## Evils of intoxication and how it becomes a social evil?

In general, one needs no introduction to know how horrible intoxication is, especially when people cannot get out of an urge in the case of chain smokers especially when they are smoking high quality vegetation, which is beyond mention, in most of our routine activities.

If that is horrible, just think what would happen if you happen to live amongst a society which bears the social evil or abuse of such intents, where everybody does that, leading to a real social dilemma, a social evil of monumental lapse.

## The Warrior "You" Francesca Terwilliger amongst all homies

But somehow, you remained as a lone warrior, trying to guide people in your neighbourhood and addressing all of their concerns, their wants, when they needed medical help, you were there to take them to the hospitals, extend attentive care to some of them, put some in rehabilitation centres and support them physically, mentally and financially. Wow you are a warrior, an angel, and an evangelist, and a... God knows what.

But life that is not easy for you, life is not that easy?

Because overnight they made you into a Borough Clerk?

Now for the onlookers let us see what a Borough Clerk does?

Appointed by the Mayor and Council, the Borough Clerk serves as the secretary of the Governing body where he or she prepares the meeting agenda, minutes of the meeting with Mayor and other councillors are prepared, resolutions as in processes including ordinances adopted by the Mayor and Council in lieu with State directives, missions, and statutes.

Also, the custodian of Municipal seal and of all the contracts, minutes, books, and records of the municipality, he or she in a Borough Clerk role acts as a liaison between the public and the Governing body, representing the Borough in relations with Local, State, and Federal governments.

But again, life for You is not getting any easier. It starts to get even harder for you.

It was way easier before becoming one such Borough clerk, where you were living life for you and your nuclear family, when you were living it when as a home dweller, life remained predictable.

But now...

Now you are a Borough clerk and not any ordinary Clerk, you have to write it out, the script that makes you think what needs to be done to accomplish your daily milestones, your little successes and your little failures in the Borough life, is what keeps coming back at you and those scripts that you write make others rely on for their day-to-day accomplishments.

The harsh realities in life revolves around you.

You are a fully functional Borough Clerk in your Borough or the neighbourhood.

Now people listen to you of what is spoken about subjects that most matter to them, hours, and hours of public intellectual intercourse that you cannot take a break at or take a few minutes recess off.

That is when you wished, whether you could nod, like what they say, Homer sometimes nods, now more like a homeless.

We understand this not because we are a clerk ourselves in any Borough of stature but understanding your position, it gives us a moment to think, when all these nodding or naps started, let us venture a little into that, so that if that is the break you longed, that is also explained on your behalf, making you a full-time warrior, a champion of public causes.

**The route that Homer took when he nods or takes naps**

To go into the subject of when Homer takes naps or during when he wandered away from subjects that required his attention, not very many references lie in journals like the National Review.  But in 2002, in one of the articles, there was a mention of it, the term Homer takes naps was again used in the journal, metaphorically or in a context which provided exposure in a niche market, alluding to a journey or in a path which were inspired by the epics including Homerian epics, Odyssey included. This presence of it again may be in one article or several but it definitely was a unique expression so that it got figured in its usage of how important taking naps were when in a meeting with public interests on one hand and the responses to it on the other.

Now considering overall the impact such an action by Homer took on the public, is yet another way to ponder into the specifics; and that would mean, something has to be settled here to say whether Homer lived in a pluralistic society?

The most direct answer to that may be a no but let us again try to get to the point of why a definite no can be said to know a little bit about the society that Homer lived in.

Homer though some argue is a term used for a society of oral poets, in fact lived in Archaic Greek society.  This was more tribal in nature and was dissected into a lot of small but competitive city-states or poleis, each with its own Gods, rulers, and customs.

The society was largely homogenous in nature with Greek ethnicity, religious worship of Olympian Gods and dialects of Greek in heavy usage in the so-called poleis.

Though Homer's Iliad and Odyssey describes a wide range of people and characters and their social formations when he describes Trojans, Ethiopians, Egyptians, or Phoenicians these mythical characters that evolve from him are mere descriptions of distant cultures, not a standing example of domestic pluralistic societies which Homer was part of.

No, It is a definite no, when you say Homer lived in a pluralistic society and for questions like whether Homer was Omer or a homie to some extent is be left out to be a subject of a different but intense discussion which are quite outside the scope of current discussions.

Here we are talking of what happens or may be the significance of Homer's naps during or while handling critical and important meetings?

So, the phrase "going on Homer nods route" most probably indicates that there is a grammatical convention in Greek language of neuter plural subjects taking singular verbs, a rule which is very different from English grammar where in English as you might know, plural subjects require plural verbs.

For instance, in Homeric Greek a sentence like The Gifts is on the table would be correct grammatically because gifts is a neuter plural subject paired with a verb, though it is absolutely left to the listener or supporter to say that thyself went for a nap and did not quite hear gifts but was only awake to hear just how gift-Ed was kept on the table.

Therefore, in essence, to indicate going on the Homer nods route would mean to suggest whether humorously or critically on someone, when they use singular verbs in the context of plural subjects, which is usually or in most cases are critically seen by the English.

So, Homer nods sometimes like a homeless goes in context to, at the minimum indicate you wholeheartedly win the support of most homeless though a sleeping homeless is not that useful in terms of any ongoing or future criticism from the perspective of grammatic correctness.

In usage, it surely lauds a useless support if it is from a homeless due to inadequate documentation; in terms of mandates or favours or a preferential liking as a public exercise in context lies the clerical work in Borough though as a Borough clerk you still cannot afford to approve lapses in the grammatical usages.

# 4

## Man cannot live by bread alone

If reports from the magazine Yorkshire Life are to be believed, in the year 2012, Yorkshire in England experienced a severe influx of immigrants (refugees) reflecting broader national trends in the United Kingdom.

The United Kingdom saw a net immigration of around two hundred thousand (two lakhs) of people though some decline (in the refugee inflow) was experienced in the immigration matter, of around fifty thousand (half a lakh) less than the previous years.

Despite the decline, immigration remained a driving factor in population growth (the growth of population) across different regions of the UK, including in counties like the Yorkshire.

If population estimates are to be believed, Yorkshire's and Humber's non-UK born population grew by 78%, particularly in the city limits of Leads, and Hull.

Mostly from Eastern Europe, regions (counties) like Yorkshire attracted refugees from all around where men started flowing into the region, in search of bread and butter.

To note, this influx of the refugee population may have contributed to changes in its demography, and may have altered the Census and Resources department's first estimates of reassessments and its study of the region's financial and economical makeup.

As per some study conducted to take a lead of situations that emerged, it was found out that there was in existence a notable increase in the refugee count from Eastern Europe, particularly from Poland and other EU accession countries.

Some noticed a significant jump in the Category of "White Other" in the undocumented class of refugees in the numerous mensural reports that were run as a result of these developments.

This is to be contrasted against an existing or documented working class that was once in existence in several counties in the UK, including Yorkshire, that is when one understands that there already are non-white folks contributing 7% in these cities like the Yorkshire, from the South Asian communities.

That would mean, overall, if a South Asian's opinion alerted 7% of the Yorkshire population, fair alerts from an Eastern European refugee or a Middle Eastern refugee alerted an easy 20% of the resultant population in Yorkshire.

So, migration of refugees was a big problem in counties like the Yorkshire of what it faced in the UK during 2012 was bearable but what was unbearable were the ongoing skirmish and the nasty and verbal, altercations that the refugee community got themselves involved in, in their attempts to blend with the local population resulting in the Administration running background checks, framing cases against hate crimes on the existing minorities in such counties.

This in turn resulted in a spike in racial proliferations of the propaganda against the loyal minorities, loyal to the monarchy but was preposterous and resulted in the detainment of several of such personals who were just but owners of a skewed mindset found themselves taking the blame for the influx in refugee population.

That is to say, when cities in the United Kingdom, like Leeds or Bradford and Hull (Kingston upon Hull) experienced ruthless refugees from the Middle East or Eastern Europe contributing to religious polarization of the refugee and the resultant populace and religious usurp; traditional and lawful migrants from South Asia were largely seen to support anything but the English due to the propaganda against the Loyalists (supporters of the British crown).

To say, contributions of South Asians to the erst British Empire in terms of its culture, living style, arts, literature, are very many and various and may require an entire folder if not a work in itself which is quite beyond the scope of this one.

But as existing in any parts of the world, racially polarized people when driven by religious extremism and innocent people from a mixed-racial makeup, stood out excellent in day-to-day business affairs picturizing unique blends in culinary habits and innovations, who introduced innovations and hence, modifications of the local cuisine protagonists were featured by the media by far as owners of abundant wisdom.

And then it happened...

In 2012 in the county of Yorkshire, people were affected by a mass hysteria and due more to the panic that resulted, many fell victims to a wave of food poisoning and experienced all the symptoms of it including diarrhoea, vomiting, nausea, and many even were hospitalized.

There was a notable food-borne illness which was developing as an incident in Yorkshire.  It was later confirmed to be an outbreak of Listeriosis and affected close to a dozen individuals across England with a significant number of them, in the Yorkshire county.

Associated with the consumption of pork-pies, the contaminant was later found out to be Listeria monocytogenes, a bacterium that caused severe illness especially in the ones that have a health condition and also in older adults.

Most of the infected ones were old people in their sixties.

The Pork-pies were believed to be purchased from several retailers in South Yorkshire and the product seemed to be supplied by a producer from that area.

So, now food safety in the UK had to be alerted to the extent, many local ones started inventing and improvising ways to obtain one of the basic necessities of life, that is food itself.

## Inventions in local food habits

The intent was conveyed in a few easy words but the actual intent were inventions in local food habits that make the locals sway away from processed food items like the Pork-pies.

In the October edition of Yorkshire Life in 2012, an article was featured about a Yorkshire resident who attempted to live on bread alone.

This endeavour was not to be treated as a dietary experiment but more like a forward-looking statement which is to be taken as a profound statement on sustainability, self-sufficiency, and a critique of modern food systems.

Concentrating on primitive and fundamental aspects of food production, it was reported that the man grew his own wheat, baked his own bread, and aimed thus to reduce his own dependence on the industrial food systems, and the corporation's weeds.

In a sense, it is not much of an exaggeration that the man did not like food that was supplied by the corporation, and made available in the cities of the Yorkshire County, mostly processed food like the Pork-pies.

Later he was seen to convey his message to the public that same year, where he said that he may make his survival instincts on home-made wheat, a regular activity, where he thought the process inculcated an inspiration that is so deeper that it remained an appreciation of his food habits that it challenged its real place of origin.

This new found wisdom and undertaking though may sound revolutionary in fact promoted Community bakeries in the Yorkshire locality, keeping traction on local food movements by gradually encouraging the public to move away from processed food items like the Pork-pies.

Slowly the traditional food items and its food sources were more controlled by these local food movements that were spearheaded by the new local people reclaiming control of the numerous food sources dictate in other words food habits for a region like the Yorkshire.

In summary, the Yorkshire resident's decision to attempt living on home grown wheat and home processed bread alone was surely an endeavour promoting self-sufficiency at a tangent lying the contemporary food systems in deep chasm.

## But he cannot live without it?

The saying, but he cannot live without it, without what?

Somebody already was of the opinion that a Man cannot live by bread alone but he assuredly cannot live without it.

Taking a historical look at John Buchan's 1927 novel, Witch Wood, the context is set about right.  This line is spoken by a character discussing the motivations of a soldier and their nature of affairs in such matters.

In this passage, the character is making its importance felt which are nothing but practical needs of individuals, particularly soldiers who require financial compensation and sustenance tactics in just about anywhere he squiggles.

Therefore, some have already said it, to refer to the essentials they are very crucial for existence in life be it food or money or the soldier who doodles and at-least when one speaks about its existence, both are way beyond a mere spiritual or an ideological existence.

# 5

## A Dole, a dime and then a penny

A few passages are dealt here which may give us in a way a solid foundation of a claim that we often hear which is not to throw away your valuables to the ones who do not appreciate them or to the ones who are not in a position to handle them well, just as in the saying, Do not throw pearls to swine.

**Pilgrim of Perfection blocks infinite bliss**

In the year 1526, the work titled Pilgrim of Perfection saw light. Published in 1526, it was a spiritual treatise attributed to William Bonde, a priest of the Bridgettine order (monk) of Syon Abbey.

Pilgrim of Perfection, a work that got released in the year 1526 is a religious, and devotional work which is notable and which reflects the moral and spiritual concerns of England in the 16th century, in the context of late medieval Catholic piety before the English reformation after which the Protestant faith was gathering ground in England.

The work, Pilgrim of Perfection is mentioned as the one in which the holy fathers were not disclosing secret mistress to every worldly man of those days.

Pearls before swine indeed...

But in actuality, the correct interpretation given to that statement from the holy fathers may be that during 1526, whoever were spiritual leaders or early Christian mystics did not disclose secret mistresses to worldly men, secret mistresses is interpreted as mystical secrets of contemplative knowledge of a higher standing that was kept as a secret in the clergy.

This phrase in particular which is "not disclosing secret mistresses to every worldly man" is a reflection of a common theme in early Renaissance mystical theology or in medieval times where the mystical secrets were not to be shared with the ones who were spiritually not prepared to accept them.

According to the Holy fathers, some of these worldly men lacked spiritual readiness, were incapable of protecting sacred knowledge, often had pride or were the ones who misused pride.

By spiritual readiness, it was noted that the worldly man was lacking purity of heart and detachment from worldly disorders that made them not spiritually ready to accept secret mistresses (knowledge).

The journey inward, it was told, was more seen as a gradual journey through the spiritual plateau requiring humility, grace, and discipline which most of the worldly men did not display.

It is a well-known thing that the early Christian mystics (Desert fathers) often withdrew from the world and shared insights only with the ones under their spiritual guidance and not as a matter of being curious individuals or being the subject of idle singles.

In short as a modern analogist cites and draws a parallel to contemplative theology, of what it is like mastering advanced physics which are understood not by many, in the same way contemplative theology is understood only by very few who have progressed through purification and illumination and who rightfully understand the unitive path or the path of the mystics.

Is there another way to look at it?

Not in the 15th century England but as we speak about the present time in India, there is another way to look at these interesting topics.  Yes, there may be ways to learn these theological subjects and advanced physics for the common man in India.

Now about learning it, to what extent it remains as pearls before swine is left to the undertaker of such initiatives, in the broader world, to quote, both the subjects are available for the interested to master, only a dedication and a strong will would get them there.

But let's also not forget that the modern learning always gives the worldly man a chance to understand and practice the contemplative theology and advanced physics so long as technically they follow whatever is required as a matter of practice, for helpful guidance some amount of trust should be with the ones whose idealism is seen to survive across the many voices amidst their dwindling beliefs.

## English Reformation in the 16th century

In England during the 16th century, English Reformation happened and the Protestant faith started gaining ground replacing Catholicism as the state religion.

What happened during the English Reformation?

English reformation was a series of events that led the Church of England break authority with the Pope and the Roman Catholic church.

Protestant reformation during that time was happening across Europe and was having a strange but a broader hold in England.

The key turning points of the English Reformation are its Acts of Supremacy where King Henry VIII declared himself as the supreme Head of the Church of England rejecting Pope's authority.  When one sees it, it was more a political move from his majesty's political franchise that was seen largely in response to Pope's refusal to annul his marriage to Catherine of Aragon.

Dissolution of Monasteries happened next where Henry shut down England's monasteries and seized their wealth and land.  This minimized the rightful living and existence of those Catholics in England as well as got themselves dismantled, all their religious beliefs and social life in England.

Under Edward VI, Henry's son in all of England's churches, Latin mass was replaced with English services and the Book of Common prayer was introduced.

Relics and images were removed from the churches in England and clerical celibacy was abolished.

Even-though during the reign of Mary I, Catholicism staged a comeback in England where many saw many of the Protestants prosecuted (Marian Martyrs), that did not last long, and  under Queen Elizabeth I, Protestantism was re-established.

In short, after English Reformation, Roman Catholicism was suppressed in England and many Catholics were subjected to Penal Laws, prosecuted, and could not hold any official positions in England.

## Lord Elgin and the Parthenon marbles

The next parable exposes Lord Elgin (Thomas Bruce) and his role as an Ambassador in Greece under the Ottoman Empire in the early 19th century where his adventures with Parthenon marbles that he took it from the Greeks using a Firman (permit) was brought to England and ultimately sold to the British Museum.

Between 1801 and 1812, Lord Elgin removed around half of the surviving sculptures from Parthenon and other sites in Athens and that included Frieze panels, metopes, and pediment sculptures.

So, if one asks whether Elgin thinks the Turks or Greeks were swine and unworthy of marbles?

The right answer may be dependent on the fact whether England in the 18th century was able to handle such an adventurous effort from Elgin, he being a spot or not.

So, the usage, marbles to Swine is a double-edged sword here. On one side, we see whether the Greeks really deserved those very marbles from their own sites since at that time they were under the Ottoman empire, who had less regard for them, and on the other side of the coin, lies Britain, who was able to handle such an artifact being in their country knowing fully well that it belonged to Greece and not Turkey.

In Elgin's mind what was playing might have been the thought that taking Parthenon marbles to Britain is not theft, but rescue of them since the Ottoman Turks did not have a favourable attitude towards Greece or their treasures, during then.

However, this view is not shared by all and even today, Greece has demanded Parthenon marbles to be returned to them despite Britain's arguments that they are preserved well in Britain and are more accessible there.

## What the Baby-boomers and Generation X put together could not handle?

An article in the Spectator magazine in the year 2001 revealed that Victorian fiction like the work: The Way of All Flesh was seen as culturally way ahead of the times.

Written by Samuel Butler and published in the year 1903, it is often cited as culturally and socially ahead of its time and has a lot of modern significance and relevance.

It is definitely forward thinking in its criticisms of the Victorian society and of the religion the people followed during those times and is a semi-autobiographical work keeping in mind the Victorian middle-class families and of their Anglican religious upbringing.

Throughout this book (work), what stands criticised is the hypocrisy, rigidity, and the repressive nature of the Victorian social values, and morality.

It attaches dogmatic religious principles stifling genuine spirituality, and individuality.

It explores self-realization and individual's freedom.

So, this work, looks like has a lot on the positive side of things, especially for a rebel in oneself, with no clear understanding on whose side the work takes side with.

Butler's novel, The Way of All Flesh is a semi-autobiographical exploration of the Pontifex family and keeps the focus on an Ernest who navigates crude societal expectations, and oppressive familial obligations, thereby severely criticising religion, education, and family.

Ernest's journey involves rejecting these institutions in favour of autonomy which is personal and goes on favouring self-discovery reflecting Butler's advocacy for individualistic bigotry over traditional survival based on a family setup and background.

## A Call for drastic changes in the year 2001

This novel encourages its readers to challenge established norms in the contemporary living and of its Victorian value system.

The expectation that is conveyed to the readers is a revolutionary and critical examination of current societal structures and the promotion of the individual agency.

Questioning class distinctions, and social mobility, the novel is seen to be critical of patriarchal authority in their rigid family structures.

Unlike many Victorian models, Butler's novel is satirical, unflinching, and candid and does not idealize family and religion at the same time.

Anticipating modern literature's realism and scepticism, its tones still resonate with today on the issues of religious doubt, personal authenticity, and family conflicts.

Throughout this work, what is kept as an ongoing debate is Tradition versus Modernity and by far this work is seen as a precursor to modern psychological novels and a literary work but on a rebellious note to the Victorian norms.

While no single book has taken on the role of the book: The way of All Flesh in the early twenty-first century, some works like White Teeth (Zadie Smith) which challenges multi-culturalism and identity and, Atonement (Ian Mc-Evan) which explores truth, morality, and complexity of human relationships, exist.

On the philosophical side, authors like Slavoj Zizek, and Alain de Botton engage in and keep alive contemporary thoughts and cultural criticisms.

<u>Events that have unfolded as a result</u>

In the year 2001, in the public domain, several events unfolded that showcased how a shift towards individualism was breaking walls with an otherwise well housed societal norm that was traditional and in line with the contemporary beliefs.

United Kingdom in that year 2001, experienced several social and cultural developments, notably Oldham riots (South Asian riots) and the racial tensions followed throughout the entire country, as a result.

Oldham riots highlighted underlying ethnic tensions in the United Kingdom and in the subsequent Ritchie and Cantle reports, some points identified included issues like lack of integration and segregation to be the cause of traditional community structures failing to address the needs and wants of a diverse society.

Round about the same time, the UK media began exploring themes around individual identity, and diversity more openly.

Under the rainbow banner, ITV's Valentine's day hosted a gay wedding which marked a significant but new moment in the lives of LGBTQ+ identifying a new place for them on the peripherals of the mainstream society.

**Challenges faced by the English mainstream society**

The mainstream societies in England and Wales did notice a lot of moral diversions from the mainstream (ways of living) which almost challenged moral, religious, and familial conventions of the Victorian societies which they were roughly adhering to until some decades ago and the deviation from them left the Baby-boomers and Generation-X in a state of mind where they started questioning institutional and familial authorities.

Many of them eventually started rejecting the Victorian morals and value systems at a more personal or psychological level and started embracing monolithic and middle eastern religion which were increasingly making inroads into the English mainstream families.

Several churches in England stopped offering their daily services and prayers and in their places of worship started opening business interests with an intent of selling ancient artifacts, and invaluable murals.

Altogether in the year 2001, the effects of violent outbursts of public anger revolutionized some parts of the English society and as mentioned under the influence of works like the Butler's work: The Way of All Flesh got themselves awakened to the rebellious outlook of their current generation.

This is to be read alongside the fact that the current generation in England forced the mainstream English society started to tread alongside paths that their older generation spited or shun to travel even though the older English generations were knowledgeable about it and of where it would take them in the not so distinct future.

# 6

## Earnings amid yearnings of sort

Movies are entertainers in a big way that the public subscribes, for both entertainment purposes, and some very few for gaining knowledge that remain unsold through the usual educational channels.

When The Last Brickmaker in America was released, no body realized that it was going to be the last television movie of the famed artist, Sidney Poitier.

Like in any movie that makes one think, this one also had its storyline set in an average household in the American suburbs and talked beautifully about the demise or vanishing away of the conventional brick building industry in the USA.

**American TV Movie – The Last Brickmaker in America**

Set in a small American town, this film closely follows one Henry Cobb a character played by Sidney Poitier, a master brickmaker who spent 57 years crafting home-made bricks at his family run brickyard.  In the story after his wife Dorothy's (cast by Mary Alice) death, Henry loses his passion for his work, especially during a time, when the town adopts machine made bricks.  This puts him back in penury.

But his life takes a turn when a 13-year-old boy by name Danny Potter (cast by Cody Newton), a troubled boy from a broken home is assigned to get help from Henry for his work on his project at school.

Through their shared work and labour, Henry becomes a mentor to Danny, teaching Danny not just brick making work but also resilience and life lessons on family and the responsibility he should shoulder for making ends meet.

In general, the characters portrayed in such TV movies convey the real-life parallels of how responsible some characters indeed are in real life who try to do work, some technical work to its perfection, and then what lies commendable is the extra care that they take in giving that something to all their dependents, and friends.

Next, we will skim through an intent in one of the PG Woodhouse characters, in Inimitable Jeeves, a character by the name of Bingo Little and what he tries to do which is to impress the lovely workers that he gets accustomed with. This gives us a chance to contrast a character study of Bingo though in the comedy world, which some argue has elements of callous and carefree attitudes towards life bundled with demonstrative aspects in guess work.

## Bingo had a bad Goodwood

In Inimitable Jeeves, P.G Woodhouse draws a classical example of character study in his analysis of the character, Bingo Little and of what the character ends up doing in his attempt to impress a woman, a recurring theme in

Wodehouse's comedy world of idle aristocrats, and their romantic misadventures.

Here in this work, Bingo Little, who is Bertie Wooster's hopelessly romantic friend, now falls in love everywhere in the world, and tries to adapt himself sometimes financially so that he gets into the shoes of a lover of these innocent girls who also happen to be doing odd jobs such as working as a waitress, other-times as a guard, with self-protection in mind.

In this story, title: Bingo has a Goodwood, Bingo falls in love with a waitress named, Mary Burgess, who is modest of all means.  Bingo in a misguided effort to appear serious, and suitable for her, tries to live a life of frugality, and embraces a working man's life, in an effort to impress her.

He begins to eat modest meals and talks about living essentially saving money as part of the act to show he is in tune with the values of an honest work and thrift.  But as many does not know that this is all an act of Bingo, he is still very much a spoilt man trying to play with people who is penurious.

## Charles Dickens and a bleak house

In the year 1853, in Bleak House, a work by Charles Dickens, he refers to the idea of saving five pounds in the context of a legal case affecting poor brickmakers.  This in one way mocks the so-called charity, shown by upper class in terms of their intervention in poor people's life, and draws a picture, full of criticisms mentioning the hypocrisy and futility of legal and social charity.

In one of the passages in this work: Bleak House, Esther Summerson's visit to a brickmaker's cottage is with a Mrs. Pardiggle, a character who satirizes aggressive philanthropy and its buildup of self-righteousness and its makeup.

Mrs. Pardiggle is a philanthropist and is a friend of Mrs. Jellyby. Mrs. Pardiggle is acquainted with Mr. Jarndyce who keeps on disliking her. In Mrs. Pardiggle's visits to the house of a brickmaker, Jenny's husband, whom she is trying to convert into her religion, although, she, a Mrs. Pardiggle, claims that she visits the brickmaker and reads to him from the Bible simply for his own good and is seen to bully and condescend in her attitudes towards the brickmaker's family. She turns a deaf ear to the family's situations and does not do anything to improve their situation.

In another scene, Mrs. Pardiggle is seen to force her five children to participate in charitable causes, started by her. In the management and handling of financial matters, she remains the sole authority and does not allow her children to give money to the suffering people. While in Britain, she does not care about the brickmaker's family and she uses all avenues of charity at her disposal as an outlet for her boundless energy, and for forcing people around her to think like what she thinks.

In one scene, Mrs. Pardiggle is seen to drag Esther into the miserable hoe of the brickmaker and his family, preaching about religion, and morality while ignoring the family's real situation in poverty-stricken situation where many people in that family suffer from diseases, sickness and hunger.

At one point there is a mention of how five pounds had been saved to get the father out of prison.  By making this statement, Charles Dickens conveys dark irony where the family is shown to be in wretched poverty and the systems that are meant to help the family rather than addressing the root causes of their suffering is seen to dazzle into exploitative labour, lack of social support, and injustice that is seen everywhere, in matters pertaining to that family.

Throughout this work, Charles Dickens uses these anecdotes to criticise institutional charity that is disconnected from the human needs, highlights the futility of bureaucratic, and legal systems especially Chancery and in most cases of Chancery, these are seen to defeat the purposes of compassion, and justice.  It also emphasises a gap between well-meant reformers and the realities that they try to serve in societies where many poor people live.

In other words, saving five pounds, has become a symbol of empty gestures, where a small amount of money is apparently thrown at the poor to get fame and a name of that of a saviour who alleviated a poor family's suffering, and these money one should remember is still thrown at the face of a few of them, pictured as classical examples of a vast but horrible human suffering.

Now we bring one's attention to another remotest place in South Asia, which is Afghanistan, and as noted, most people belong to tribes in Afghanistan and are considered poor by all means, which means many suffer there from poverty and neglect.  Even-though under the current administration, the basic (living standards) has improved, the people of Afghanistan as a country have to go a long way to acquire living standards of an under-developing country or a developing country that has got it going for its citizens.

## Cave complex of Gandhar in Ancient India

The cave complex of an ancient kingdom in South Asia, called "Gandhara", also called as Gandhar, refers not to a single cave complex but to a region that is broad in ancient India, now situated in Pakistan, and in the eastern part of Afghanistan, that played a crucial role in the development of Buddhist learning, architecture, and arts, in the 1st Century BC to the 5th Century AD.

Gandhara, as a kingdom was situated in the valleys of the rivers, Kabul, and Swat and flows through important cities in those regions, which are Purushapura (Peshawar in Pakistan), and Taxila (pronounced Taksha-sila).

It used to serve as cross-roads between Indian, Central Asian, Greek, and Persian cultures and contributed significantly to a unique and influential religious tradition and in art forms and style, to the most advanced in those ancient days.

While Gandhara is not known for elaborate and sophisticated cave complexes as what we see in the present-day India, but it has several rock-cut monasteries and stupas carved into cliffs, and hillocks often used by the ancient and the present-day Buddhist monks.

In analysing ancient artforms and sculptures from this region, a few places stand out in ancient Gandhara, including Jamal Garhi in Mardan district in Pakistan where features of Buddhist monastery and stupa are in existence, Takht-i-Bahi which is a UNESCO world heritage site, and Shahbaz-Garhi which contains Ashoka's edicts described in Kharosthi script.

Gandhara was very famous for the ground-breaking inventions of the Gandhara school of Art, which is said to have blended Indian artistic traditions, and Hellenistic (Greek) artistic traditions.  It is said that these art forms were the first ones in the world, to have depicted Lord Buddha in human form, inspired from Greek sculpture gods like the Appollo.

This region also has a lot of stone reliefs showing scenes of Buddha's life, Jataka tales, and figures with Hellenistic features, and clothing.

Believed to be the place, which was ruled by Gandhari's father, Subala, Gandhar, a region that is in present day Pakistan, and Afghanistan, is believed to be ruled by him in ancient day India.

Subala is also known for being the father of Sakuni, who was Gandhari's brother, who played a significant role in the Mahabharata epic, as an advisor, and instigator on the side of the Kauravas.

In the epic, Mahabharata, there is also mention of Dhritarashtra, who is the husband of Gandhari and, whose father was Veda Vyasa (compiler of the Vedas), and mother, Ambika, one of the queens of King Vichitravirya.

Dhritarashtra though blind, where his blindness is often seen as a symbol of his moral, and spiritual blindness towards his son's wrong doings, is said to have fathered a hundred son known as Kauravas.

He is also often criticised for his inability to control his ambitious son Duryodhana, for failing to act justly when needed, by going blindly by the books, especially when playing the Chathuranga which resulted finally in the humiliation of Draupadi, the Pandava's wife.

This ultimately resulted in Kurukshetra war, which was a war fought between the Pandavas, and Kauravas mentioned in the Mahabharata epic.

Now it is made known to everyone that somebody is interested in knowing if there ever was, a demolition of these Cave Complexes, in Gandhara, by the rulers of Gandhara in the 19th century, Afghanistan.

Some of the ancient Buddhist cave complexes and monuments in Afghanistan including the ones with the Gandharan heritage suffered demolition, and destruction in the early to late 19th century, although the most notorious demolitions happened in the 20th and the 21st centuries.

In the 19th century, Afghanistan was caught in the middle of a political struggle of the Great Game between the British, and the Russian empires. During this period, there were demolition of Buddhist caves known for its historical importance, as well as the intentional demolition of the Buddhist sites, especially stupas, and caves, looted for relics, and artwork by the European treasure hunters of during those times.

After the demolition, the remaining stones and bricks were used by the local population for repurposing including building homes, and forts, and some even used it for construction work to slow soil erosion, etc.

More direct destruction of the Buddhist caves happened in the 21st century, in terms of destruction of Bamiyan Buddha, which was destroyed by the Taliban, the stupas dating back to the 6th century AD. The Bamiyan cave complex, which surrounded these statues included hundreds of monastic cells, paintings, and murals, and many of them were also deteriorated or damaged due to the ongoing conflicts during that time in Afghanistan.

Recently there were reports of destruction and damage to Buddhist stupas and related heritage sites in Afghanistan in the Tap-e-Sardar shrine near a place called Ghazni, where a 7th century Buddhist shrine was demolished or partly damaged by the Taliban's religious police.  This action is in alliance with the group's long-standing policies of destroying artifacts which are everything which is pre-Islamist or before the Islamic period in Afghanistan.

Despite these destructive actions by the Taliban's religious police, the Taliban administration has made contradictory statements which is supportive of their efforts in protecting the ancient Buddhist city of Mes-Aynak during the underground operations, that were held in the region. These days, they have also opened the site of the destroyed Bamiyan Buddha shrines to tourist and charge an entry fee to the tourist who may visit these sites.

## Tora Bora and the dreaded terrorists

Tora Bora in Pashtun means Black Cave and it is a rugged mountainous region in the Eastern Afghanistan, located in Nangarhar Province which is bordering with Pakistan.  The area is said to be covered with natural caves, and tunnels.

Back in the war with the Soviets, or during the cold war, this area was fortified by the Mujahideen during the Soviet-Afghan war in the 1980 turning this area into a military stronghold between opposing forces.

This complex due to the way of the natural habitat offered protection from aerial attacks and high-altitude terrain was very difficult for the infantry to fight in this region.  It provided as a natural aqueduct or may just be a duct for the ones, that offered easy escape routes into Pakistan's tribal areas.

After the Soviet-Afghan war got over in the mid to late 1980s, this area was prone to a lot of fighters and the area became volatile or susceptible and began to subsume a war-torn climate.

After the World Trade attacks (9/11 attacks) on the US by the terrorists, the US launched operation, Enduring Freedom in October 2001 to dismantle al-Qaeda, and remove Taliban from wielding power in Afghanistan.

US Intelligence indicated that the 9/11 master mind Osama Bin Laden and his associates had taken refuge in the Cave complex in Tora Bora, and hence since US decided to use its Special forces, and its CIA operatives to forge into alliances with the Northern Alliance and tribal military, they launched an assault and attacked the area in Tora Bora.

Now here again, there are a few interesting questions, on the Afghan war of 2001, the questions specifically on the weaponry that the US military or its alliance used in Afghanistan that were used to demolish the caves in Tora Bora and about whether any detonators were used in the operations to demolish the Tora Bora caves?

The answer to which is...

Yes, there may be detonators used in the Afghan war in the year 2001 and it was used to demolish the Tora Bora Cave complex.

During the early phase of the US led invasion of Afghanistan after the 9/11 attacks, Tora Bora in eastern Afghanistan became a key battleground since the US believed that the master mind of 9/11 attacks on the US was hiding out in that region.

The cave complex in Tora Bora was a natural and fortified rock network, reportedly built up with bunkers and tunnels, and sophisticated weaponry was required from the US side to make demolition attempts on the ancient cave network in Tora Bora.

The weapons used were the Precision-Guided Munitions or PGMs including laser guided bombs, and GPS-guided Joint Direct Attack Munitions, which were delivered primarily by the B-51 and B-1B bombers as well as by the F-15s and F-16s.  The main goal for the attacking force (US force) was to strike at the entrance of the caves, cave mouths, and suspected underground bunkers.

Another tool used was Bunker Busters, which is one of the most sophisticated weaponries using GBU-2B, and GBU-37 bunker busting bombs. These are deep penetration munitions and pierces hardened underground facilities before detonation, as for instance, GBU-28 which is a 5000-pound laser guided bomb with enough and more power to dig into the rock and soil after demolition of the cave complexes.

Possibly, Thermobaric weaponry was also used to destroy the caves, where typically these weapons use a two-stage explosion to detonate a cave, on one phase it disperses a cloud of fuel and another phase it ignites it creating overpressure ideal for the destruction of enclosed spaces like in a tunnel.  It is not officially confirmed by the US, but its use may have been a possibility in the detonation and destruction of the Cave complex in Tora Bora.

Detonators like JDAMs or GBU bunker busters were also used as a fusing mechanism to control when a particular bomb explodes, for instance when it explodes as in on contact or after penetration of the cave, or in the midway when in the cave during an airburst.

**Tight control on coverage of Afghan war**

On December 6th, 2001, the front page of Washington Post prominently featured the headline: Tight Control marks coverage of Afghan war.  This article in a detailed manner discussed the restrictions that were stringent and were imposed on the journalists covering the US Military operations in Afghanistan, particularly highlighting the limited access restricting those reporters with their ability to inform about the events and happenings on ground or directly from the site. This piece of article highlighted about press freedom and transparency during the early days of the Afghan war.

Also on the same day, the Washington Post reported this in its news article, with title: Ashcroft defends Anti-Terrorism steps, in which Attorney General John D Ashcroft defended the Justice department's post on 9/11 Anti-Terrorism measures before a Senate Committee and argued that these steps were essential for national security suggesting any criticism of them may aid the terrorist's causes.

## What do I buy with it?

Trade wars bring in a fresh new perspective to the countries participating in trade and brings in added revenue in terms of levies charged in form tax collected on certain items which is a lot of income to the government who is levying taxes, and the tax covers a lot of products that go as part of international trade.

The most important thing is that the goods traded are with countries that have plenty to offer and fosters at some level or another, a lot of trading activity which in the long run gives way to innovation, and enhancing living standards in the countries engaged in such trading activities despite in situations where a trade war is in force, and sometimes not.

But involving in perilous activities with a poor country who have nothing to offer and destruction of its vast cultural assets presents a no-win-win situation to any country let alone the poor country who may be dependent on income from may be tourism when it sees its cultural assets destroyed presenting no income from such operations as opposed to the engaging country who may spent millions in war operations with the poor country, only fostering hostile climate and instability in the region, in return gets no trading activity from the poor.

So, it is after all, wise to go with the extended paraphrase, do not spent a lot on military operations against poor countries, when emotionally they need the support of the dominating power...

Always remember, a penny saved is a penny earned...

The same conditions more or less existed while in a discussion regarding Canterbury Tales or Canterbury Guests, well which one is not sure, but in the year 1695, Edward Ravenscroft's play carried a comment and conveyed it in The Canterbury Guests or the play titled, A Bargain Broken, which stood show at the Theatre Royal in Drury Lane in September 1694...

The comment went like this, "This I did to prevent expenses for a penny saved is a penny earned..." and appears in Act II, Scene 4 in the play.  In this scene, Sir Buffler Barnaby explained his decision to bring along his brother and sister while arranging for a marriage, and he told it is to bring down the lodging expenses.

This impromptu makes one wonder in the European markets and elsewhere, whatever was done by the Enron team, to reduce expenses so that it may have averted the depreciation of its stocks value and not make it fall off from its face value, plummeting the stocks trade for a penny.

So, the question is, what it may have meant for its employees who were keeping a stash of the company stocks in the belief that it would go up.  Some even may have tried to save their life earnings in that stock.  Don't you think it is preposterous of why the Enron plummeted to such low levels?  Let us examine...

## The Enron Scandal

In 2001, the Washington Post has run a story and uncovered the personal impact of the Enron Scandal on individuals, particularly focused on a former employee who suffered significant financial losses.

One notable story involved a George Maddox, a former plant engineer, who at 78, lost around $1.3 million in retirement savings due to Enron company's collapse. As a result of this, he had to return to work somewhere in rural East Texas, mowing pastures to survive and make ends meet.  This account like many others is from real life heroes and their determined come back underscoring the lasting and profound effects that a scandal of Enron's nature had on the lives of its employees.

## Family circus in Washington Post

It was interesting to see that in Family circus on December 6, 2001, illustrated by Washington Post had a strip which mentioned about an old adage: A penny saved is a penny earned.  It was more a child's interpretation of the adage and how his innocence led to the complete misunderstanding of the proverb, offering a light-hearted reflection on how normally children misinterpret and perceive expressions used by the adults.

It was more a direct response from Jeff, who thought it is ok to have a penny but what should he buy with it.

This innocent question makes one think about a child's literal interpretations of the world-market emphasizing how limited it is in scope when it is bound to nose-dive and when all one sees is that the pretty bullions in paper become a worthless penny.

This comic strip that day also illustrated family circus at its best where a child's perception brought in fresh and amusing takes on an expression which had gone out of control when conceptualizing about the financial world.

This is also a light-hearted reflection on the gap between a child's understanding of money value and the financial wisdom that is sometimes borrowed by the adults who may be handling their own personal financial markets, without knowing the economic impact which they contribute towards, as a result of their action.

# 7

## Penny wise and pound foolish

If you refuse to make a small financial outlay for instance to repair or insure (quote from 1864), you may find yourself faced with having to make a very larger one.

The quotation is from the year 1864 and sounds more like superstitious.  However, the adage is truthful in its essentials, that if you not try to solve your problems that which can be solved by a needle, like a knitwear, you end up having to solve it using a spade, like mowing or performing a manicure.

### Science, Superstitions, and horses

To expand on this headline, one needs to be aware of what it is, when somebody talks about The Piedmont Hunt. Readers be aware, there is nothing superstitious about it but there may be elements of science and yes horses when one talks about The Piedmont Hunt.

So, what it is?

The Piedmont Hunt is a traditional fox hunting club based in the State of Virginia, in the USA.  It is one of the oldest and most prestigious of all fox hunting operations organized in the United States, with its roots dating back to the late 19th century or the early 20th.  This club specializes in organizing hunts where riders on the horseback follows a pack of hounds by tracing the scent of a fox, which usually is mastered on a trained scent trail and the hunters become successful by practicing this activity (sensing the scent of foxes) where the activity by itself is steeped in the countryside sports and tradition.

The location of this fox hunting operations conducted by this club lies in the Piedmont region of Virginia, an area well known for its rural landscapes and the rolling hills.

Activities seem to sprawl in this neighbourhood whenever The Piedmont Hunt happens, if in better form remains the social events that centre around this activity, in best form goes the organized fox hunts, and the equestrian sports.

The culture if one may ask is British, and is part of a broader tradition of fox hunting in the US, reflecting historical ties to the British hunting customs in the backdrop of an aristocratic but rural society.

The members of this club may include landowners from the area, fans of rural outdoor activities and sports, and may also be the equestrians from the area.

A master and huntsman of a hunt, like the Piedmont Hunt manages the hounds, organizes hunts, maintains the traditions of the club, and is in fact in a position, where the position gets called in a key leadership role, as a leader or a key leader.

Yes, Randy Waterman served as the Master and Huntsman of the Piedmont Hunt in Virginia, during the late 1990s into the early 2000. In 1998, a tragic barn fire destroyed a structure on Waterman's Clifton Farm in Loudoun County, and it resulted in a loss for him of ten thoroughbred racehorses and 15 hounds used at The Piedmont Hunt. Despite all of this, the family members, farm workers, and firefighters who was called upon to help, rescued numerous hounds, and four horses from the blaze set forth then.

Now for the ones believing in superstitions, one can adhere to the saying, an old proverb which says Penny wise and Pound foolish.

As it was in 1864, when Mrs. Henry Wood wrote Trevlyn Hold, that the idea of insuring a home or not doing so carried importance due to the very risk that normal households face during the Victorian (era) time-period.

Even though there were numerous perils associated with not insuring home, it was generally believed that Fire, and Storm or Weather damage to some extent can be compensated when one insures the home.

When Mrs. Wood writes that a man would never insure a home, she may be telling that because of a sense of carelessness or fatalism, a general distrust in insurance companies or may be a matter of one's own prudence, foresight or a personal choice.

Whatever reasons, the superstitious might have stayed away on a foresight that may have prompted many not to insure, despite the warnings from works or stories in the late 17th Century (when the Sun Fire Office started) including Mrs. H Wood complaining on ricks that catches fire when sunburnt, a decision that makes a Penny wise and a Pound foolish.

Now some superstitions about the horses...

In 1607, Edward Topsell an English cleric and author, published the title: The History of Four-Footed Beasts.

It is a comprehensive zoological work that complies knowledge from various sources, including the work by Conrad Gessner (Historiae Animalium).

It is said that Topsell's work is notable for its elaborate engravings such as the famous depiction of the rhinoceros, based on woodcut by Albrecht Durer, about his empirical observations with mythological and anecdotal events providing valuable insight into the historical perspective on animal lives.

For the superstitious, it is mentioned in his work but not as a superstition, that whenever horses withdrawing from their ordinary food, it is an indication from an animal's behaiour as omens or reflections of moral or a supernatural phenomenon.

It is ideally not clear that in the case of Randy Waterman that the horses exhibited a similar behaviour the previous day of inferno which might have been indicative of a carnage of those beasts engulfed by a conflagration or a holocaust but the superstitious never let it go and keep indicating of its existence.

## Piedmont Hunt and a Randy Waterman

In 1999, Randy Waterman faced felony charges for a hit-and-run charge related to a serious accident involving Dr. William Katz, who was a prominent physician from Upperville. On April 25, 1999, when the incident occurred,

Waterman allegedly waited for three hours reporting his involvement in the accident. This delay raised questions and concerns among the hunt members about damages to the relationship with landowners who usually allows the hunt to take place in their property.  That same year, the judge did not forego the hit-and-run case implicating Randy Waterman on his involvement in the hit-and-run case.

**Insurance Fraud in the Victorian period**

Insurance fraud in the Victorian period was a grave concern leading to legislative reforms and public outcry.  Several high-profile cases of which one is highlighted revealing the vulnerability in the insurance from during those days.

Deptford Poisonings (1886-1889)

Amelia Winters, a woman from Deptford, insured lives of 22 individuals, many her relatives of which five of those insured died under suspicious circumstances, leading to investigations in many places.

While Amelia Winters herself died before the trial, Elizabeth Frost, her daughter was convicted of forgery for falsifying insurance documents, and was sentenced to servitude for seven years.

**Financial stability and affordability**

Talking about financial stability and affordability, what lied as a stable system in the Victorian period was foretold in a quotation from Joseph Addison's The Spectator in the year 1712.  In one of his essays, Addison criticises that women who enter into marriage without ensuring and not insuring their husbands can provide for them.

In this context, Addison uses the proverb "Penny wise and Pound Foolish" to describe women who perhaps in the pursuit of immediate emotional satisfaction, completely discount the practical considerations of financial stability in marriage.  He is of the opinion that such decisions are unwise since the priorities lie with short term gains over long term wellness.

# 8

## Duties in Marriage

Modern governments legislate in haste and repent at leisure.  This quote emerged in the Spectator on 10th January 1998 is deeply descriptive about the importance of the State when it gets associated with a larger Union. Now, this to a reasonable extent is true given an account of the way the UK Government worked in unison with the EU government despite its own share of dissident voices which still demanded complete sovereignty of the United Kingdom.

### Act in haste and it is all a waste

When asked about one's elaboration of the theme, Act in haste and it is all a waste from the perspective of the UK chairing EU Presidency in the year 1998, offered a rich ground for exploring how ill-considered or rushed into, were some of the political decisions that UK took, on behalf of EU which led to unintended consequences and missed opportunities in the delicate field of Union politics in an arena of European Union's diplomacy and policy making.

The context was right for Mr. Blair who had come to power in 1997 as British Prime-minister with a victory that was unprecedented. He positioned himself as a pro-European leader and a modernizer of the prevalent times.

Times were good for the UK to assert itself and lead the way pushing policy initiatives but then they did push it in a far too aggressive way.

The EU operated largely on a consensus basis and with less haste and pushed agenda without patent diplomacy that otherwise could have resulted in watering down any policies in terms of delay and outright rejections.

For instance, in one of the major initiatives was the UK's emphasis on social policy, and employment aiming to add a social dimension to the EU.  But since UK made haste in decision making and rushed through the changes without accounting for a divergent economic model, it left countries like Scandinavia or Germany and got them alienated in the process, which might surely have diminished the credibility of the United Kingdom.

**Legislate in haste and repent at leisure (What it means for the EU governance?)**

United Kingdom held the presidency of the Council of the European Union in 1998 during the first half of that year. This role was supposed to rotate amongst the EU members once in every six months and the UK was responsible for chairing meetings and setting agenda during that period.

The same period saw the United Kingdom taking decisions which are swift decisions without any thorough deliberation.  However, for most of these decisions, the outcome was dismal, disappointing or unfavourable.  The very language during use then indicated that UK's approach and decisions were criticised by the EU members.

## Saving fashion and tattoo, a taboo

Inspecting how the privileged societies in the European Union move and take opinions, somebody asked if Lady Diana in the first half of the twenty first century criticised in public about social habits of engraving oneself with tattoos.

It was in general a response which voiced that there existed no credible evidence that suggested Princess Diana publicly expressed an opinion about tattoos or the public interest in them.  Princess Diana was an intensely scrutinized figure, a public figure, but her commentaries typically focused on mental health, humanitarian issues, landmine crises, and creating AID awareness, and not on topics like the body art.

However, one should notice and reconsider some points regarding Royal Image and Conservatism, which during Princess Diana's time, the British Royal family was associated very much with conservative values and traditional values.  So, when the subject of tattoos was somewhat taboo in upper class and royal circles, in the years following 1980s, and if Princess Diana expressed approval of a body art, it might have stirred comment no matter what but as one knows there is no presence of such remarks in the public records or in the public domain.

Another question emerged where it was asked, if Princess Diana was an influencer of Fashion and its different norms, to which the answer given was that, Diana was a trendsetter in fashion and personal expression but she was not an influencer in the royal family or adjacent circles like Meghan Markle or Princess Eugenie.

## Festivities and participation in them

Somebody asked about festivities in the United Kingdom, and if there was a public sentiment against princesses attending festivals in the United Kingdom in the year 2002.

The short answer given was as follows...

In 2002, there was no widespread public sentiments in the UK against princesses attending events or festivals, traditionally not associated with royalty.

But due to controversies and scandals, the year 2002 was marked by significant scrutiny and declining public support for the royal family.

In reports that were published in the same year, towards November 2002, in Guardian and in an ICM poll, it was revealed that only 43% people believed that Britain would be worse off without the royal family, the lowest level of support since the tracking began which was believed to be in the year of 1987.  In addition to that, around 26% of people who were respondents to the survey expressed indifference indicating that the monarchy was felt in the light of a growing sense of irrelevance.

Despite this, or challenges like this, the Golden Jubilee celebrations that ran in June 2002 saw a resurgence in public enthusiasm, with a lot of people, believed to be close to a million people attend events in London.  This indicated that even though the monarchy faced criticism, public interest in royal events remained stronger than the previous years.

In regard to the attendance of princesses at non royal festivals, there is no evidence to suggest that such participation was always met with public criticisms.

In-fact members of the royal family including Princess Anne were recognised for their participation in public events and engagements during this period and is always marked by joyous celebrations and peaceful propriety in feelings shown in such events.

In summary, while the royal family faced public scrutiny in the year 2002, no significant backlashes existed against princesses attending events or functions outside of the royal events and traditional events.

Now we will consider a statement which sets the expectations on whether in a family circle in Britain, whether woman take a more active role than man, and whether these expectations are changing across generations.

**Duties in Marriage**

In Britain, traditionally, when one considers gender roles in the family, women are expected to take on more family and caregiving duties than their counterpart, that is the man, have been historically common, but these expectations change also across generations.

In older generations and in some cultural or religious communities, implicit or explicit expectations set women to be the managers or primary caretakers of the household.

The media portrayals and social norms from the past also indicate that idea, of woman taking on more domestic roles in the family.

However, in modern Britain, especially in the younger generations, there is a social trend towards shared responsibilities in domestic and family life.

Fathers are increasingly involved in household duties, emotional labour, and childcare and in whichever avenues where many families strive for equal division of labour.

The UK government has also introduced policies that support shared parental leave allowing both the parents to take time off after the birth of a child.

Despite all of this, research and statistics in Britain shows that women on an average do more unpaid domestic labour than their men in the United Kingdom.

In summary, in the UK today, there is no universal expectation that all family duties are to be taken care of by women, they may still do more due to a mix of lingering social norms, personal choice or structural barriers, however the cultural momentum shows, it is equal division of labour and moves towards equal participation in family matters and family duties and gets equally shared between a man and a woman in a family.

# 9

## Politics make strange bedfellows

Here, primarily we try to dissect through two notable events, which echoes the gist in the statement, Politics make strange bedfellows.  The notable events are from the year 1995, and the events of interest are available in the public domain, in the form of newspaper articles published then.

It was during 1995 that Mr John Major (also Major John) faced significant challenges within his party, due to divisions between its members over the European Union and the fallout from Back-to-Basics campaign, which was interrupted by a series of scandals.  These issues led Mr. Major to resign as the Conservative Party leader in June 1995, prompting a re-election, which he won with a sizeable majority.

Now, the second event happened in the US, with Mr. Clinton (Bill Clinton) who was the president of the USA from January 20, 1993 till January 20, 2001. Since the Republican Party was in majority in the Senate and the Congress, the mid-1990s in the US were marked by intense political developments and partisan politics including the implementation of the "Contract with America", a Republican-led initiative and ongoing debates on welfare reforms, and federal spending.

Now these events are seen from the perspective of certain elaborated paraphrases and see what the literary critique conveys on those not-so-distant political developments and of the manoeuvring sought on strictly conflicting takes by the members.

## Hyde and the Irresistible Metaphor

The phrase "Forgive the Unforgivable", from Mr. Hyde in reference to the character from Robert Louis Stevenson's Strange Case of Dr. Jekyll and Mr Hyde, symbolises the hidden side and darker side of a person.  In political discourse, invoking Mr. Hyde often suggests a figure or a leader exhibiting a dual natured person who is publicly virtuous but in private an authoritarian or a corrupt personal.

The expression "forgive the unforgivable" implies a situation where groups of individuals overlook more severe transgressions or failings, possibly for strategic positioning of themselves or for political gain that may accrue as a result.

In the context of the mid-1990s, these metaphors might have been held to place criticisms over political figures or actions that appear in morally questionable situations or in hypocritical situations that emerged then in Washington DC politics.

For instance, the ongoing debates over political partisanship versus personal morality questions thrown at President Bill Clinton in 1998, and around attempts of impeaching him exactly demonstrates the political conditioning from during that period.

## Statecraft and the Conservative crises

Peter Van Greenaway's 1980 novel, The Dissident, goes deeper into the complex political identity and the nature of opposition wielded in political circles and goes on finding middle grounds between astute politicians but in opposite campaigns prompting them to take measures that are partisan due more out of attainment of common goals as opposed to the political realm they represent.

The common goals which these politicians keep are mostly professional in nature and no one is known to falter away on the personal side with figurative nuances and daily errands.

The phrase "even enemies have something in common" encapsulates a recurring theme in Peter Van Greenaway's work with the idea that fosters a pair of ideological adversaries most often share underlying similarities in methods, and goals and very rarely in vulnerabilities that they face.

In the work, The Dissident, the protagonist a Soviet political prisoner is recruited by the KGB to pose as a defector to the west. The operations aim to expose Western world's hypocrisy by revealing the fabricated nature of narratives from dissidents, leading them to a crisis of identity and allegiance, once the defecting happens, with the protagonist becoming disillusioned with the western world's own moral contradictions, and dilemma.

The quotation reflects the novel's exploration of how western democracies, and the Soviet regimes employ similar tactics of manipulation, and control by creating propaganda stories favouring themselves contrasting ideological differences.

It underscores most of the time, the notion that the political systems, even when positioned as opposites, mirror's each-others methods and flaws. This perspective though aligns with the idea of the theorist Carl Schmitt, who posits that the distinction of a friend and enemy is central to the political identity of politicians. This is because, his arguments centre around political entities who defines themselves in opposition to others, and this antagonism is not merely a matter of ideology but of existential necessity according to him. In this light, recognizing commonalities between enemies does not diminish their opposition but rather highlights the shared structure that defines their existence.

Greenway, another proponent of this narrative invites readers to question the binary classification of us versus them by considering the complexities of political identity. It suggests that the understanding of the adversary's commonality lead to a more nuanced comprehension of human condition, and global conflicts.

But the opponents of this theory argue that the moment a political stand taken by a politician is compromised in line for a higher or a bigger political mandate, the story of the politician ends there abruptly and it is from then on, that the politician starts looking for common ground and adjustment politics which in later days has become a common happening, a mere observation.  Now, what it does to the political landscape is their systematic degradation of themselves and their ideals from the ranks of a staunch and strong leader to the underdog categories of themselves becoming first a democratic leader gradually stepping out in the open as an abode of philanthropic activism supporting various causes lacking a convincing but a moral stand.

In the case of Monica Lewinsky's statement on moral trepidation in the Oval office, during her years as a relatively low-profile White House intern in the year 1995, the scandal involving herself and President Clinton did not break until 1998.

There were no public statements, cases or media reports involving Lewinsky on or around March 31st in the year 1995.

There were no major or historical notable speeches or public statements made by President Clinton specifically on March 31st 1995.

However, what was in focus during that day was the Republican sponsored initiatives which was "Contract with America" which were a series of welfare reforms, and budget debates.

President Clinton was navigating tensions with the Republican controlled Congress but no landmark announcement or statement were made or recorded on that exact date.

Going into the details of The Contract with America, it was more a political agenda and a legislative proposal released by the Republican Party in 1994, unveiled on September 27, 1994.

The contract outlined a set of promises that the Republicans made to American voters if they won control of the US House of representatives. Crafted mainly by Newt Gingrich, who became the Speaker of the house in 1994 elections, the contract aimed to reduce government size, reduce crime, cut taxes, reform welfare, and increase government accountability were the sole aims conveyed.

Now, somebody seemed to be interested to know if there ever was an immigration crack down in the border of Texas on March 31st 1995?

The answer to that goes as follows...

Yes, there was a significant immigration enforcement operation along the Texas-Mexico border in March 1995, though it concluded by 31st of March.

The US Border Patrol initiated a two week crack down along the Texas-Mexico border and the operation when concluded, marked 50% increase in arrests, seized 10,300 pounds of Marijuana, 1.3 pounds of cocaine, 230 odd vehicles, 10 weapons and around $44540 dollars in cash.

To say, the least, the broader enforcement efforts from US Border Patrol during that period, which concluded in mid-April, was significant in the shaping of US Border security policies.

## Irony and discomfort of alliances forged

In the UK however, during 1995, the story was a little different.

There, Mr. Major John (John Major) the Prime Minister of UK's party the Conservative party was in deep crises.  They were very heavily divided, on the issue of European integration, the divide on question: Euroscpetics versus Europhiles and were suffering from a series of scandals: Tory sleaze that could not hold the public trust. This internal division and external pressure from a resurgent Labour Party under Tony Blair represented immense adversity to the government of Major John.

While John Major ultimately won the leadership contest against John Redwood, who had resigned his post of a Cabinet minister to contest, the mere act of having a sitting Prime Minister be challenged by a Cabinet minister highlighted extreme divisions which were internal to the party.

It meant ideological opponents, who might tolerate each other for the sake of party unity, were not openly against each other.  The party as a whole was forced into a situation where its members despite their deep disagreements had to align themselves even if temporarily to avert a situation and resolve any impending leadership issues.

The outcome though a victory for Major John, did not fully heal the divisions and the party remained unpopular eventually leading to their defeat in the year of 1997.

## Party Politics and Poverty

In 1839, P Hone in his Diary notes on 9th July commented that party politics like poverty bring men, acquainted with strange bedfellows.  P Hone was an Irish diarist and politician known for his keen political and social commentaries. His diary entries provided insights into the early 19th century social dynamics in the political culture.

Party politics often forces individuals or groups of individuals with different value system and beliefs to work together towards a common goal, sometimes the members work sleazily and reluctantly to the attainment of goals owe to these differences.

Poverty, similarly, can force people into uneasy and unexpected alliances which most use for their own survival and improvement of their conditions.

In this context, while explaining the adage or quote: Politics make strange bedfellows, strange bedfellows would mean unlikely or uncomfortable partnerships.

However, in the broader context, both politics and poverty may create situations where pragmatism overrides ideological differences and personal preferences.

It highlights how external pressure whether economic hardship or political competition lead one to form alliances that might seem entirely contradictory or quite at odds with the belief system one adheres.

In short, our discussion may have covered, well established variants of adversity make strange bedfellows, which has thus far explained, adversity from the perspective of hardship, challenges or difficulties and bedfellows from the perspective of unusual or unlikely alliances to overcome a common problem or a threat.

# 10

## Put up or shut up

(The Last Communication from self-styled leaders)

"Now if he means business, let him put up or shut up, for this is the last communication that will come from me in regard to this fellow".

Self-style leaders and boxers like John Morrissey might have made this statement directed against his rival, John Heenan, in the year 1858 but its relevance is surely felt in a more flamboyant way, when the leaders do still want business to go on as usual, despite an existence of them enlighten the crowd, the spectators, or remain as mere echoes across the formidable depths.

### What is business as usual in Marysville (Ohio) in 1858?

The business as usual in Marysville (Ohio) in 1858 was the usual, the talk on money, to be put up as a stake for the match.  John Morrissey was very clear in his message to John Heenan, either you put up the stake money so that the boxer fight can go on, repenting any mention of boxing as a means and end to fighting that may go on, or just shut up and leave him alone.

The significance of this statement made in the year 1858 is profound due the reasons that it is the earliest recorded use of a common idiom, which is put up or shut up in published print.

Also, one has to be really up with the wits, to know if the stakes for the match, involved anything beyond money, may be inclusive lies the bare necessities of life, is a question in itself.

This usage of put up or shut up was formidable when one inspects the origin in pugilism or gambling where many things are offered as stakes in the context of a boxing challenge, it then becomes crucial understanding the phrase's original meaning.

Put up though it may sound as if it means to live with another self, it most probably in the Ohio context, may indicate referring to putting money up for a wager or a stake as in a fight or a game.  If one is truly confident in one's abilities or claims, one will put one's money in support of an argument or as a wager to a fighting sequence.

In America, during the 1800s, this shows the mentality of those Americans then, where they preferred a speedy resolution to a problem, rather than talking endless and aimlessly about it.

So, the people from Ohio those days, reflected a conversation style which was more direct, matter of fatedly, a no-nonsense approach to disputes and its resolution, by opening a channel to fight, perfectly encapsulating that spirt which goes for decisive actions over prolonged unproductive discussions.

While its roots are specific to the world of boxing and gambling, this usage in the year 1858 demonstrates how quickly it gets accepted into the broader language.  It simply means, Prove your claims with concrete action or stop making those claims.

On top, it also gives a perspective on how public challenges and disputes were conducted in the mid-19th century, often through pronouncements made in the newspapers, or through letters send to public officials through a postal office and their means.

It is generally expected from during those days that the individual who is making such statements, stands up to it when questioned in public or when asked to wager a fight on those silly topics.

**What is Mr. Major John's put up or shut up challenge in his political leadership meetings in 1995?**

There was a parallel and strong correlation that existed between John Major's "put up or shut up" leadership challenge in 1995 and the sentiments that were expressed in a 1995 article in the Washington Times.

The quote began with quote: Adversity makes strange bedfellows and then went on with it until it culminated in unquote: Put up or Shut up challenges in the Conservative party line-ups in Britain.

Major's decision to resign as party leader but not as Prime Minister and his decision to immediately stand for re-election was a big gamble.  He challenged his critics within the party line-up to either put up with the show or shut up so that a downer syndrome (pity) runs through its rank to the relegated member.

This act itself was in response to the adversity that he faced, and the dissident this time had to succumb despite the other, John, mounting a coarser but terse opposition from within the party line, found the soil running lose owe to Major's strongest presence.

In summary, the quotation perfectly encapsulated the fractured and tumultuous political landscape in Britain during John Major's leadership challenge in the year 1995. It spoke with confidence to the desperate circumventers that forced unlikely confrontations and reveal an uncomfortable alliance or the lack that was not until that time visible in the Conservative Party lines or line-ups.

**What the UK Takeover code meant for Stryker in 2014?**

The quote was very relevant in the handling of those dreaded take over missions circumventing or trying to go along with that line on the UK Takeover Code's PUSU (put up or shut up) rule.  In 2014 it was on Stryker, which is a US based company, considering a takeover of a UK entity which was Smith & Nephew and the take-over did not occur. Even though, more details of this take-over bid were not known to a lot of people, it is speculated that it might have been because of the PUSU rule that they were unable to renew bids on Smith & Nephew.

<u>How PUSU works</u>

The PUSU rule is designed in such a way that it prevents Phantom Bids or prolonged uncertainty that has the potential to damage the target company.  It aims to ensure that the bidders or the bidders in the potential list make a committed offer that which is formal or withdraw explicitly allowing the target to get back to business without the constant threats of a takeover.

The way it works is if a company makes a public announcement of a possible offer to take over another one, or if the rumours become so specific then the Takeover panel which is the Regulatory authority in UK overseeing takeovers allows the potential bidder to either, Put up: in which case the company interested should make the offer or Shut up: in which case the company is prohibited from making an offer for takeover for another six months.

In 2014, Stryker was widely rumoured to be making an offer of takeover to acquire Smith & Nephew, a major UK based medical technology company, but the offer of takeover did not go through, and its details are not known or is not available in the public domain for any literary review.

# 11

## See no Evil, Hear no Evil, Speak no Evil

"You can ... squeeze your eyes shut like a child in a storm, determined to, see no evil, hear no evil, speak no evil and still that evil storm may come at you with hands like knives one day".

This quote generates some kind of an apprehension on the onlookers, who may be devastated after a tornado or its smaller forms of a stronger wind that might have struck the United Kingdom in the year 2013 on December 13th, the system of storms called as Xaver.

Not an year later, there was yet another storm that struck the United Kingdom and this time they wasted no time but to name it Abigail, the fiercest storm system to have struck the UK.

Storm Abigail was the first named storm of the 2014-2015 season, bringing with it heavy rainfall and strong winds and caused localized flooding, travel disruptions, and power outages particularly in Northern Ireland and in Scotland.

While the UK itself has a rich history of superstitions, in particular in their rural areas, there is no evidence to suggest that superstitious activities were there to have contributed to the events after the storms struck the small towns in the year 2014.

Now there is already a curious question from one corner who kept asking about Abigail, the biblical character and what authority and influence she holds on the Thirteen colonies in British North America?

That seemed to be a fare question since even when Abigail is a revered biblical character, she is also perceived to be a character involved in many references in sorcery and in the Salem witch hunt time frames of the many stories that may have emerged from there.

So, the portrayal of Abigail has a lot of historical and literary connotations when one studies about the Thirteen colonies in British North America and in the context of the Salem witch hunt trials and her representation literarily in the Arthur Miller's The Crucible.

In the Bible, Abigail is depicted as a virtuous and wise woman.  She is the wife of Nabal, a wealthy but a foolish man, and then she later marries King David.  Her story is found in 1 Samuel 25, at times when David starts taking vengeance on her household, she is pictured as a person who intervenes demonstrating foresight and diplomacy.

The biblical Abigail is celebrated for her beauty, intelligence, and integrity including her moral integrity.

Now when we take a look at Abigail Williams, she is portrayed as a villainess, a cast that would make her a literary villain.  She was associated with the Salem Witch hunt trials in the year 1692 and was a 12-year-old niece of Reverend Sameul Parris.  She and her cousin Betty Parris, exhibited strange behaviours that led to the accusation of witchcraft.  Abigail's role was very significant in the Salem Witch Hunt trials because she was one of the leading accusers, and her actions contributed to the individuals, in fact several individuals who got executed.

In Arthur Miller's 1953 play, The Crucible, Abigail Williams is portrayed as a manipulative character and has vengeance written all over her. Miller's Abigail is driven by a desire for power, and jealousy, particularly in her pursuit of John Proctor.

To know John Proctor is similar to knowing a character who is a complex, tragic protagonist, a farmer in the Puritan town of Salem, Massachusetts during the time of the Salem Witch Hunt trials.

While Abigail Williams was not a sorceress, the Salem Witch Hunt trials were deeply rooted in the Puritan belief in the supernatural forces that were in play during that time, and henceforth.

In short, the story of Abigail Williams, both as a literary figure, and a historical figure serves as a cautionary tale about the dangers of abusing power, mass hysteria, and the consequence of unchecked authority, highlighting its importance and relevance to the contemporary issues of morality and justice.

# Epilogue

<u>Rare sighting of salvation, sanctification, and forgiveness</u>

This book as you might have noticed, begins with a feeling of compassion over the fact how we as humans are destined in so many ways, contented were the experience felt by a Francesca Terwilliger in all her different reincarnations, who was also flabbergasted and startled when she got herself exposed both physically and mentally is quite one thing to be taken note of.

On the contrary, playing spectators to her show, what went unfamiliar were thoughts of a genuine pearl, in fact when she was on the seat, a rare sight, despite all the hullaballoo that she as in the toon character, a Francesca Terwilliger made up in each of her appearance, quite a maverick, evident we feel the exhaustion in her extempore shows.

Almost the same feeling can be gathered by the Reader, in the concluding chapters of this book, where an event or a happening is described in all its finesse, arising of unfaithful alliances both politically or for that matter for some, personally, that lead the bearer or their dependent to be the subject of a public wager in the (United) states.

The wager decided what sort of punishment was given by the larger public sentiments in the States to the bearer or their dependent who were involved in this unfaithful alliance, whatever the wager's outcome was, decided or culminated in the actions of a Striker from Ohio, who delivered it on the bearer or their unfaithful half.

In the final chapters again, the hit definitely was on the nephew or niece and nobody is spared when one reads with contempt the golden words, that "Nobody is above Law", even when the sovereign is trapped in a web of deceit in a forgotten island by questionable characters who evaded (Law) and fell, and then turned out to be web-stained.

This book which is a rare sighting of getting exposed, reminds us all of the First exposure in 1999 in the States, which led the naked truth become more clearer in the public domain, where the world trade of a State meant not worldly trade and in public eyes in the States, the sale of a State's real estate was not going to become a secret ordeal, anymore.